Fantasy Science Field Trips

A Visit to a Space Station

Claire Throp

Chicago, Illinois

Edited by Dan Nunn and Catherine Veitch
Designed by Cynthia Akiyoshi
Picture research by Ruth Blair
Production by Vicki Fitzgerald
Originated by Capstone Global Library Limited
Printed and bound in China

17 16 15 14 13
10 9 8 7 6 5 4 3 2 1

Library of Congress Cataloging-in-Publication Data
Throp, Claire.
A Visit to a space station / Claire Throp.
    pages cm.—(Fantasy field trips)
Includes bibliographical references and index.
ISBN 978-1-4109-6197-6 (hardback)—ISBN 978-1-4109-6202-7
(paperback) 1. Space stations—Juvenile literature. I. Title.

TL797.15.T47 2014
629.44'2—dc23   2013012665

Acknowledgments
We would like to thank the following for permission to reproduce
photographs: Corbis p. 19 (© NASA/Reuters); ESA pp. 11, 21, 23, 25,
26, 28; Gagarin Cosmonaut Training Center p. 6; Getty Images pp.
8 (Sergei Remezov/AFP), 9 (Bill Ingalls/NASA); NASA pp. 12, 14, 15,
16, 18; Science Photo Library pp. 13, 24 (NASA), 20 (CHASSENET/
BSIP); Superstock pp. 4 and title page (Science and Society), 5
rocket, 17 (Ben Cooper/Science Faction), 5 child (Blend Images),
7 (StockTrek Images/Purestock), 10, 22, 25 (StockTrek Images), 27
(dieKleinert), 29 (Science Photo Library).

Cover photograph of an astronaut reproduced with permission of
Shutterstock (© iurii).

Every effort has been made to contact copyright holders of
material reproduced in this book. Any omissions will be rectified in
subsequent printings if notice is given to the publisher.

Some words are shown in bold, **like this**.
You can find out what they mean by
looking in the glossary.

Contents

Let's Take a Trip to a Space Station

Space stations stay in space for many years. People go there to live and work for four to six months. Let's take a trip to the **International Space Station (ISS)**. Put on your space suit and get ready to blast off.

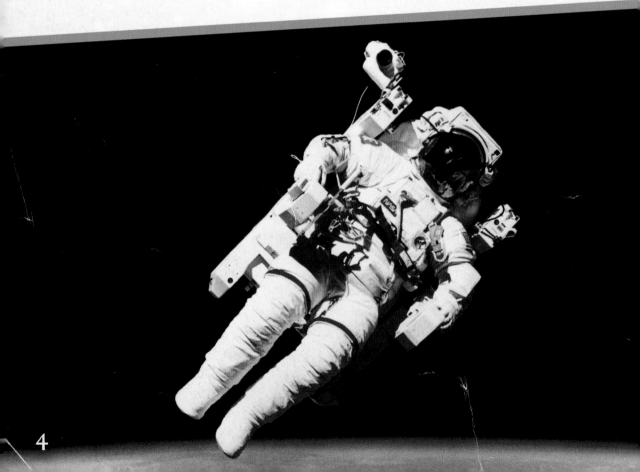

Be Prepared

Gravity is the force that holds us to the ground when we are on Earth. There is very little gravity on a **space station**. This means that if something—or someone—is not tied down, it floats away. You'll need to do some hard training before we go.

Moving in water is a good way to train for walking in space.

Astronauts are attached to the space station while working on it. Otherwise, they would float away into space!

Liftoff!

To get to the **space station**, we have to travel in a Russian *Soyuz* spacecraft. **Astronauts** strap themselves into special seats because there is very little room to move around.

Make sure you are comfortable, because this journey will take two days!

The journey to the space station takes longer than the return to Earth. This is because it takes awhile for any spaceship to catch up with the moving space station.

Arrival

We have arrived! Our spacecraft links with the **space station** at a **docking port**. Once the spacecraft is locked on, doors called hatches open to allow us into the space station.

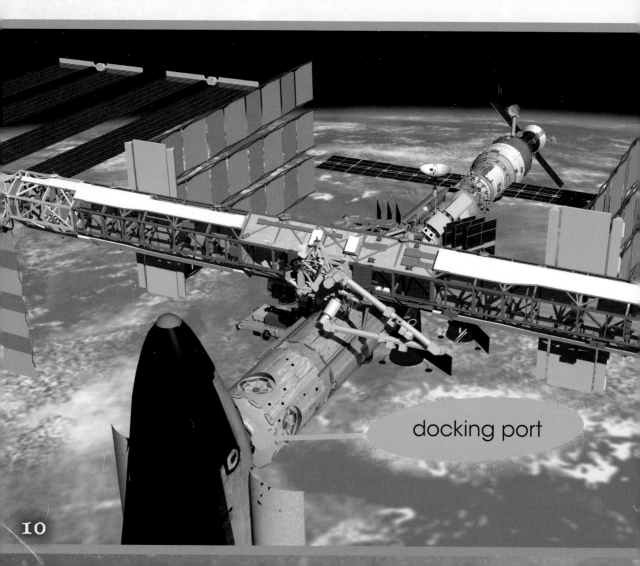

docking port

This part of the space station is called Zarya.

Everyday Life

Astronauts sleep in sleep stations about the size of a refrigerator. Astronauts cannot take showers, because the water would float away. Many astronauts use wipes and dry shampoo instead.

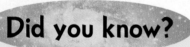
Did you know?

Astronauts sneeze about 100 times a day! This is because dust does not settle on a surface as it does in our homes. It floats in the air.

Space stations have special toilets. Toilet waste is sucked up like a vacuum cleaner sucks up dirt.

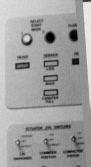

ACCESS PANEL

It's dinnertime! The food on a **space station** is **dehydrated**. This means it has had water removed so that it can stay fresh longer. **Astronauts** add water to the food so they can eat it.

Other food on space stations is in packages that just need to be heated up.

Did you know?

Some astronauts eat with trays of food strapped to their legs! If it was not attached to them, the food would float away.

Supplies

The **European Space Agency's (ESA)** Automated Transfer Vehicle (ATV) is used to take **supplies** to the **space station** about once a year. This includes fuel, equipment, and food.

Did you know?

After about six months, the ATV is used to take away waste from the space station.

Supplies are kept in spaces under the floor and in the walls.

Free Time

Astronauts on a **space station** have time off from work, just like we do on Earth. Some play musical instruments. Others may play games or watch movies. They also all get time to talk to their family or friends back on Earth.

The **cupola** is an area where astronauts can see Earth through a large window.

Exercise

Astronauts have to exercise on a **space station** to keep their muscles healthy. Because there is very little **gravity**, astronauts don't use their legs much. Their leg and back muscles become weak.

Experts check the astronauts to make sure they are healthy.

Did you know?

Astronauts on the **ISS** exercise for about two hours every day.

Work

To keep the **space station** in good working order, repairs and checks need to be carried out. **Astronauts** working on the outside are attached to the station by a safety line called a **tether**.

tether

On **space walks**, astronauts wear a jet pack. This means they can return to the space station using the powered jet pack if the tether breaks.

tether

jet pack

Some **astronauts** have the job of taking photographs of the **space station**, Earth, the Sun, and space. This can be done from inside the space station or outside.

Did you know?

The **ISS** is more than 200 miles above Earth. That is about the same distance as New York City to Boston.

photograph of the space station taken by an astronaut

Science in Space

Scientists carry out experiments in **laboratories** on board the **ISS**. They test different materials such as metal and liquids to see how they behave in space. Scientists also see how living in space affects people's bodies.

This is Columbus, a science laboratory on board the ISS.

Back to Earth

It is time to blast back down to Earth. Returning to Earth after six months can be tough. Some **astronauts** have trouble standing up because it can take awhile to adjust.

Several countries have worked together to build the **ISS**. It has taken many missions to take all the parts out and attach them together in space.

Glossary

astronaut someone who is specially trained to work in space

cupola area on the ISS where astronauts can see Earth through a large window

dehydrated dried from having water removed

docking port place where a spacecraft joins with a space station by locking onto it

European Space Agency (ESA) organization that runs the European space program

gravity force that attracts things to the center of Earth

International Space Station (ISS) space station built by a number of different countries

laboratory room where scientific tests can be carried out

space station large structure that stays in space for a long time. People can live and work there.

space walk time an astronaut spends outside a space station in space

supplies stock or store of something such as food

tether safety line that attaches an astronaut to the space station when he or she is working outside it

Find Out More

Books

Dowswell, Paul. *First Encyclopedia of Space*.
  Tulsa, Okla.: EDC, 2010.
Graham, Ian. *The Best Book of Spaceships*.
  New York: Kingfisher, 2007.
Hunter, Nick. *Space* (Explorer Tales).
  Chicago: Raintree, 2013.
Tagliaferro, Linda. *Who Walks in Space?: Working in
  Space* (Wild Work). Chicago: Raintree, 2011.

Web sites

FactHound offers a safe, fun way to find web sites
related to this book. All the sites on FactHound
have been researched by our staff.

Here's all you do:
Visit **www.facthound.com**
Type in this code: 9781410961976

Index